slow cooking

MARKS &
SPENCER

Marks and Spencer p.l.c.
PO Box 3339
Chester CH99 9QS

shop online
www.marksandspencer.com

ISBN: 978-1-907428-28-9

Printed and bound in China

slow
cooking

contents

taking it slow

There are many wonderful things about slow-cooked food: the delicious, comforting aromas that fill the house, the fact that you don't need to spend hours in the kitchen on preparation and the idea that you can create crowd-pleasing meals with very little effort.

The recipes in this book – for soups, stews, casseroles, curries, roasts and even desserts – have one thing in common: they all benefit from long, slow cooking. Because of that, many of them use the cheaper cuts of meat that are most delicious when cooked slowly and gently for a long time, emerging succulent and melt-in-the-mouth.

In the slow cooker

Slow cookers are perfect for meals that practically prepare themselves. You simply place all the ingredients in your slow cooker, turn it on and leave it bubbling away while you get on with other things.

We used a 4.5-litre slow cooker, the most popular size, for our recipes. If you have a smaller or larger slow cooker you may need to increase or decrease the quantity of ingredients and, almost certainly, the amount of liquid you use.

Always follow the manufacturer's instructions and safety guidelines when using your slow cooker.

Cooking on the hob and in the oven

The best type of pot to use is a heavy-based casserole dish as this will contain and spread the heat evenly. Make sure the lid fits the dish tightly or, to really seal in the flavours, you can cover the dish with a layer of wet, crumpled parchment paper and place the casserole lid on top.

When you're cooking in the oven, as with slow-cooking on the hob, the best choice is a heavy-based casserole dish that will radiate the oven's heat throughout the pot.

Slow-cooking less expensive meat

When you're using cheaper cuts of meat, you should remove the excess fat and large pieces of gristle but the smaller connective tissues will break down and help thicken and flavour the sauce.

Cut across the grain of the meat where possible when you are dicing it and always brown it first – this is the key to giving the sauce more flavour and a rich colour.

in the slow cooker

LAMB SHANK, FENNEL & VEGETABLE SOUP

prep + cook time 10½ hours **serves** 6

1 tablespoon olive oil
4 french-trimmed lamb
shanks (1kg)
1 medium brown onion (150g),
chopped coarsely
2 baby fennel bulbs (260g),
sliced thinly
2 medium carrots (240g),
chopped coarsely
4 cloves garlic, crushed
2 fresh small red thai chillies,
chopped finely
2 teaspoons ground cumin
2 teaspoons ground coriander
1 teaspoon ground cinnamon
1 teaspoon caraway seeds
pinch saffron threads
1.5 litres (6 cups) water
2 cups (500ml) beef stock
400g canned chopped tomatoes
400g canned chickpeas,
rinsed, drained
¼ cup (90g) frozen petit pois
1 cup loosely packed fresh
coriander leaves

1 Heat half the oil in large frying pan; cook lamb, until browned all over, then place in 4.5-litre slow cooker.
2 Heat remaining oil in same pan; cook onion, fennel, carrot, garlic and chilli, stirring, until onion softens. Add spices; cook, stirring, until fragrant. Place vegetable mixture into cooker. Stir in the water, stock, undrained tomatoes and chickpeas. Cook, covered, on low, 10 hours.
3 Remove lamb from cooker. When cool enough to handle, remove meat from bones, shred meat; discard bones. Stir meat, peas and coriander leaves into cooker. Season to taste.

nutritional count per serving 6.1g total fat (1.4g saturated fat); 953kJ (228 cal); 13.6g carbohydrate; 26.3g protein; 6.7g fibre

suitable to freeze at the end of step 2

BORSCHT

prep + cook time 8 hours 50 minutes serves 6

60g butter
2 medium brown onions (300g),
chopped finely
500g beef braising steak, cut
into large chunks
1 cup (250ml) water
750g beetroot, peeled,
chopped finely
2 medium potatoes (400g),
chopped finely
2 medium carrots (240g),
chopped finely
4 small (360g) tomatoes,
chopped finely
1 litre (4 cups) beef stock
⅓ cup (80ml) red wine vinegar
3 bay leaves
4 cups (320g) finely shredded
cabbage
2 tablespoons coarsely chopped
fresh flat-leaf parsley
½ cup (120g) soured cream

1 Melt half the butter in large frying pan; cook onion, stirring, until soft. Place onion in 4.5-litre slow cooker. Melt remaining butter in same pan; cook beef, stirring, until browned all over. Place beef in cooker. Add the water to the same pan; bring to the boil, then add beetroot, potato, carrot, tomato, stock, vinegar and bay leaves to slow cooker. Cook, covered, on low, 8 hours.
2 Discard bay leaves. Remove beef from soup; shred using two forks. Return beef to soup with cabbage; cook, covered, on high, about 20 minutes or until cabbage is wilted. Stir in parsley.
3 Serve soup topped with soured cream.

nutritional count per serving 20.6g total fat (12.4g saturated fat); 1689kJ (404 cal); 25.3g carbohydrate; 25.3g protein; 8.8g fibre

suitable to freeze at the end of step 1

SPICY RED LENTIL & CHICKPEA SOUP

prep + cook time 6 hours 20 minutes **serves** 6

2 teaspoons vegetable oil
1 medium brown onion (150g),
chopped finely
2 cloves garlic, crushed
2.5cm piece fresh ginger
(15g), grated
2 teaspoons smoked paprika
1 teaspoon ground cumin
½ teaspoon dried chilli flakes
375g butternut squash,
chopped coarsely
1 stalk celery (150g), trimmed,
sliced thickly
¾ cup (150g) red lentils
400g canned chickpeas,
rinsed, drained
400g canned chopped tomatoes
3 cups (750ml) water
3 cups (750ml) vegetable stock
⅓ cup (80ml) finely chopped
fresh flat-leaf parsley

1 Heat oil in small frying pan; cook onion, garlic and ginger, stirring, until onion softens. Add spices and chilli; cook, stirring, until fragrant.
2 Place onion mixture into 4.5-litre slow cooker; stir in squash, celery, lentils, chickpeas, undrained tomatoes, the water and stock. Cook, covered, on low, 6 hours. Season to taste.
3 Serve soup sprinkled with parsley.

nutritional count per serving 3.9g total fat (0.8g saturated fat); 815kJ (195 cal); 23.5g carbohydrate; 12.4g protein; 7.9g fibre

suitable to freeze at the end of step 2

ITALIAN CHICKEN SOUP

prep + cook time 9 hours **serves** 6

1.5kg chicken
3 large tomatoes (650g)
1 medium brown onion (150g),
chopped coarsely
2 stalks celery (300g), trimmed,
chopped coarsely
1 large carrot (180g),
chopped coarsely
2 bay leaves
4 cloves garlic, peeled, halved
6 black peppercorns
2 litres (8 cups) water
¼ cup (155g) orzo pasta
½ cup coarsely chopped fresh
flat-leaf parsley
½ cup coarsely chopped fresh basil
2 tablespoons finely chopped
fresh oregano
¼ cup (60ml) fresh lemon juice

1 Discard as much skin as possible from chicken. Chop 1 tomato coarsely; chop remaining tomatoes finely, refrigerate, covered, until required.

2 Place chicken, coarsely chopped tomato, onion, celery, carrot, bay leaves, garlic, peppercorns and the water in 4.5-litre slow cooker. Cook, covered, on low, 8 hours.

3 Carefully remove chicken from cooker. Strain broth through fine sieve into large heatproof bowl; discard solids. Skim and discard any fat from broth. Return broth to cooker; add orzo and finely chopped tomatoes. Cook, covered, on high, about 30 minutes or until risoni is tender.

4 Meanwhile, when cool enough to handle, remove meat from bones; shred coarsely. Discard bones. Add chicken, herbs and juice to soup; cook, covered, on high, 5 minutes. Season to taste.

nutritional count per serving 14.1g total fat (4.4g saturated fat); 1580kJ (378 cal); 23.2g carbohydrate; 37g protein; 4.5g fibre

suitable to freeze at the end of step 2

PUMPKIN SOUP

prep + cook time 6½ hours serves 6

30g butter
1 tablespoon olive oil
1 large leek (500g), sliced thinly
1.8kg piece pumpkin or butternut
squash, chopped coarsely
1 large potato (300g),
chopped coarsely
3 cups (750ml) chicken stock
3 cups (750ml) water
½ cup (125ml) pouring cream
1 tablespoon finely chopped
fresh chives

1 Heat butter and oil in large frying pan; cook leek, stirring, until soft.

2 Combine leek, pumpkin, potato, stock and the water in 4.5-litre slow cooker. Cook, covered, on low, 6 hours.

3 Cool soup 10 minutes. Blend or process soup, in batches, until smooth. Return soup to cooker. Cook, covered, on high, about 20 minutes or until hot. Stir in ⅓ cup of the cream. Season to taste.

4 Serve soup topped with remaining cream and chives.

nutritional count per serving 17.9g total fat (10.1g saturated fat); 1275kJ (305 cal); 24.8g carbohydrate; 9g protein; 5.1g fibre

suitable to freeze to at the end of step 2

BALSAMIC & PORT BEEF SHANKS

prep + cook time 8 hours 20 minutes **serves** 6

1 tablespoon olive oil
1.8kg beef shank, cut into 6 pieces
1 large red onion (300g),
sliced thickly
1 stalk celery (150g), trimmed,
sliced thickly
½ cup (125ml) beef stock
½ cup (125ml) port
¼ cup (60ml) balsamic vinegar
400g canned chopped tomatoes
2 sprigs fresh thyme
1 tablespoon light brown sugar
⅓ cup coarsely chopped fresh basil
2 teaspoons finely grated
lemon rind
½ cup (60g) pitted black olives

1 Heat oil in large frying pan; cook beef, in batches, until browned. Transfer to 4.5-litre slow cooker. Add onion, celery, stock, port, vinegar, undrained tomatoes, thyme and sugar to slow cooker; cook, covered, on low, 8 hours.
2 Stir in basil, rind and olives; season to taste. Serve beef with sauce.

nutritional count per serving 6.3g total fat (5.9g saturated fat); 1726kJ (413 cal); 12.1g carbohydrate; 48.2g protein; 1.9g fibre

suitable to freeze at the end of step 1

tips Ask the butcher to cut the beef shank into 6 equal pieces for you, or you could use 6 x 300g pieces shank of beef. Dry red wine can be used instead of port.

SALT BEEF WITH HORSERADISH SAUCE

prep + cook time 8 hours 10 minutes **serves** 6

1.5kg piece salted silverside
or brisket
1 medium brown onion (150g),
chopped coarsely
1 medium carrot (120g),
chopped coarsely
1 stalk celery (150g), trimmed,
chopped coarsely
10 black peppercorns
1 tablespoon brown malt vinegar
1 teaspoon light brown sugar
2.5 litres (10 cups) water,
approximately

horseradish sauce
45g butter
2 tablespoons plain flour
2 cups (500ml) hot milk
1 tablespoon creamed horseradish
1 tablespoon coarsely chopped
fresh flat-leaf parsley

1 Rinse beef under cold water; pat dry with absorbent paper. Place beef, onion, carrot, celery, peppercorns, vinegar and sugar in 4.5-litre slow cooker. Add enough of the water to barely cover beef. Cook, covered, on low, 8 hours.
2 Make horseradish sauce just before serving.
3 Remove beef from cooker; discard liquid and vegetables.
4 Slice beef thickly; serve with horseradish sauce and a mix of steamed seasonal vegetables: try baby potatoes, carrots, peas or beans..

horseradish sauce Melt butter in medium saucepan, add flour; cook, stirring, 1 minute. Gradually add milk, stirring, until sauce boils and thickens. Stir in creamed horseradish and parsley. Season to taste.

nutritional count per serving 26.1g total fat (13.9g saturated fat); 2266kJ (542 cal); 10.2g carbohydrate; 65.7g protein; 1.4g fibre

not suitable to freeze

tip You can buy salted beef from butchers or online.

BEEF, DATE & SPINACH TAGINE

prep + cook time 8 hours 35 minutes **serves** 6

1.2kg braising steak, chopped
coarsely
¼ cup (35g) plain flour
1 tablespoon olive oil
1 large red onion (300g),
chopped finely
2 cloves garlic, crushed
1 teaspoon ground cinnamon
1 teaspoon ground cumin
½ teaspoon ground ginger
½ teaspoon ground turmeric
¼ teaspoon saffron threads
1 cup (250ml) beef stock
400g canned chopped tomatoes
¾ cup (100g) pitted dried dates
315g spinach, shredded coarsely
1 tablespoon thinly sliced
preserved lemon rind
⅓ cup (45g) coarsely chopped
roasted unsalted pistachios

1 Toss beef in flour to coat, shake off excess. Heat half the oil in large frying pan; cook beef, in batches, until browned. Transfer to 4.5-litre slow cooker.

2 Heat remaining oil in same pan; cook onion and garlic, stirring, until onion softens. Add spices; cook, stirring, until fragrant. Add ½ cup of the stock; cook, stirring, until mixture boils.

3 Transfer onion mixture to cooker with remaining stock and undrained tomatoes; stir to combine. Cook, covered, on low, 8 hours.

4 Add dates, spinach and half the preserved lemon rind; cook, covered, on high, about 10 minutes or until spinach wilts. Season to taste.

5 Sprinkle tagine with pistachios and remaining preserved lemon rind.

nutritional count per serving 20.4g total fat (6.5g saturated fat); 1977kJ (473 cal); 22g carbohydrate; 47.5g protein; 5.6g fibre

suitable to freeze at the end of step 3

BEEF RIBS WITH STOUT & CARAMELISED ONION

prep + cook time 8½ hours **serves** 6

1 tablespoon olive oil
2.5kg racks beef short ribs
2 large brown onions (400g),
sliced thinly
1 tablespoon light brown sugar
1 tablespoon balsamic vinegar
¼ cup (60ml) water
3 medium carrots (360g),
sliced thickly
400g canned chopped tomatoes
5 sprigs fresh thyme
1 tablespoon dijon mustard
1 cup (250ml) beef stock
1 cup (250ml) stout

1 Heat half the oil in large frying pan; cook ribs, in batches, until browned. Remove from pan.
2 Heat remaining oil in large frying pan; cook onion, stirring, until soft. Add sugar, vinegar and the water; cook, stirring occasionally, about 10 minutes or until onion caramelises.
3 Transfer onion mixture to 4.5-litre slow cooker; stir in carrot, undrained tomatoes, thyme, mustard, stock and stout. Add ribs, turn to coat in sauce mixture. Cook, covered, on low, 8 hours. Season to taste.
4 Cut ribs into serving-sized pieces; serve with the sauce.

nutritional count per serving 21.4g total fat (8.1g saturated fat); 2228kJ (533 cal); 12g carbohydrate; 67.2g protein; 3.5g fibre

suitable to freeze at the end of step 3

tip For best results, get the butcher to cut the ribs into individual pieces. They become more tender and fit more easily into the slow cooker.

OSSO BUCO WITH MIXED MUSHROOMS

prep + cook time 8 hours 50 minutes **serves** 6

12 pieces veal shank
(osso buco) (1.7kg)
¼ cup (35g) plain flour
2 tablespoons olive oil
1 large brown onion (200g),
chopped coarsely
1 cup (250ml) marsala
1½ cups (375ml) beef stock
¼ cup (60ml) worcestershire sauce
2 tablespoons wholegrain mustard
2 sprigs fresh rosemary
185g chestnut mushrooms,
sliced thickly
155g portobello mushrooms,
cut into 8 wedges
155g oyster mushrooms,
chopped coarsely
½ cup (125ml) pouring cream
¼ cup (35g) gravy powder
2 tablespoons water
½ cup coarsely chopped fresh
flat-leaf parsley

1 Coat beef all over in flour, shake off excess. Heat half the oil in large frying pan; cook beef, in batches, until browned all over. Remove from pan.

2 Heat remaining oil in same pan; cook onion, stirring, until onion softens. Add marsala; bring to the boil. Add onion mixture to 4.5-litre slow cooker; stir in stock, sauce, mustard and rosemary. Place beef in cooker, fitting pieces upright and tightly packed in a single layer. Add mushrooms to cooker. Cook, covered, on low, 8 hours.

3 Carefully remove beef from cooker; cover to keep warm. Add cream and combined gravy powder and the water to cooker; cook, covered, on high, 10 minutes or until mixture thickens slightly. Stir in parsley; season to taste.

4 Serve beef with mushroom sauce and a mash – potato, celeriac or sweet potato are all good choices.

nutritional count per serving 16.5g total fat (7.1g saturated fat); 1902kJ (455 cal); 17.4g carbohydrate; 45.5g protein; 3.7g fibre

not suitable to freeze

tip You can use a mixture of mushrooms as we have, or just one variety with a good robust flavour – you need a total of 500g.

RED WINE, BEEF & MUSHROOM STEW

prep + cook time 8 hours 25 minutes **serves** 6

16 spring onions (400g)
2 tablespoons olive oil
375g button mushrooms
4 slices rindless bacon (260g),
chopped coarsely
3 cloves garlic, crushed
1 cup (250ml) dry red wine
¼ cup (70g) tomato paste
½ teaspoon caster sugar
1.2kg stewing beef,
chopped coarsely
2 medium fennel bulbs
(600g), sliced thickly
⅓ cup coarsely chopped fresh
flat-leaf parsley

1 Trim green ends from onions, leaving about 8cm of stems attached; trim roots. Heat oil in large frying pan; cook onions, mushrooms, bacon and garlic, stirring, until onion softens. Stir in wine, tomato paste and sugar; bring to the boil, boil, uncovered, 2 minutes.
2 Place beef, fennel and onion mixture in 4.5-litre slow cooker. Cook, covered, on low, 8 hours.
3 Stir in parsley; season to taste. Serve stew over creamy polenta or mashed potato; accompany with steamed green beans.

nutritional count per serving 21.3g total fat (6.8g saturated fat); 1952kJ (467 cal); 6.3g carbohydrate; 53.1g protein; 5.2g fibre

not suitable to freeze

MOROCCAN LAMB WITH SWEET POTATO & RAISINS

prep + cook time 6 hours 25 minutes **serves** 6

2 tablespoons olive oil
1.2kg boned lamb shoulder, chopped coarsely
1 large brown onion (200g), sliced thickly
4 cloves garlic, crushed
2 tablespoons ras el hanout
2 cups (500ml) chicken stock
½ cup (125ml) water
1 tablespoon honey
2 medium sweet potatoes (800g), chopped coarsely
400g canned chickpeas, rinsed, drained
1 cinnamon stick
3 cardamom pods, bruised
⅓ cup (50g) raisins, halved
½ cup loosely packed fresh coriander leaves
⅓ cup (55g) coarsely chopped blanched almonds, roasted

1 Heat half the oil in large frying pan; cook lamb, in batches, until browned all over. Remove from pan. Heat remaining oil in same pan; cook onion and garlic, stirring, until onion is soft. Add ras el hanout; cook, stirring, until fragrant. Remove from heat; stir in stock, the water and honey.

2 Place sweet potato in 4.5-litre slow cooker; stir in chickpeas, cinnamon, cardamom, lamb and onion mixture. Cook, covered, on low, 6 hours. Season to taste.

3 Stir in raisins and coriander; sprinkle with nuts to serve.

nutritional count per serving 30.5g total fat (9.7g saturated fat); 2567kJ (614 cal); 34.9g carbohydrate; 47.2g protein; 6.3g fibre

suitable to freeze at the end of step 2

HONEY SOY LAMB CHOPS

prep + cook time 6 hours 40 minutes **serves** 6

¼ cup (60ml) salt-reduced
soy sauce
¼ cup (90g) honey
3 cloves garlic, crushed
1 teaspoon sesame oil
2 large red onions (600g),
cut into thick wedges
6 lamb forequarter chops (1.2kg)
6 sprigs fresh rosemary
15g butter, melted
1 tablespoon plain flour

1 Combine sauce, honey, garlic and oil in small jug.
2 Place onion in 4.5-litre slow cooker; top with lamb, soy sauce mixture and rosemary. Cook, covered, on low, 6 hours.
3 Discard rosemary, remove lamb from cooker; cover to keep warm.
4 Combine butter and flour in small bowl; stir into cooker. Cook, covered, on high, about 25 minutes or until sauce thickens; season to taste. Strain sauce through fine sieve into medium heatproof jug; discard onion.
5 Serve lamb drizzled with sauce and accompanied with steamed salad potatoes, petit pois and carrots.

nutritional count per serving 16.9g total fat (8.2g saturated fat); 1588kJ (380cal); 19.5g carbohydrate; 36.2g protein; 1.6g fibre

suitable to freeze at the end of step 2

LAMB TAGINE WITH HARISSA & GREEN OLIVES

prep + cook time 4 hours 35 minutes **serves** 6

1.2kg boned lamb shoulder, chopped coarsely
1 large red onion (300g), grated coarsely
2 cloves garlic, crushed
2 tablespoons finely chopped coriander roots and stems
1 cinnamon stick, halved
1 teaspoon ground cumin
1 teaspoon ground ginger
1 teaspoon sweet paprika
⅓ cup (80ml) olive oil
1 tablespoon harissa
800g canned chopped tomatoes
¼ cup (70g) tomato paste
½ cup (125ml) beef stock
400g canned chickpeas, rinsed, drained
2 tablespoons honey
½ cup (90g) pitted small green olives
2 teaspoons finely chopped preserved lemon rind
½ cup loosely packed fresh mint leaves

1 Combine lamb, onion, garlic, coriander, spices and half the oil in large bowl.

2 Heat remaining oil in large frying pan; cook lamb, in batches, until browned all over. Transfer lamb to 4.5-litre slow cooker.

3 Stir harissa, undrained tomatoes, paste, stock, chickpeas and honey into cooker. Cook, covered, on low, 4 hours.

4 Remove cinnamon stick; stir in olives and lemon rind. Season to taste; sprinkle with mint.

nutritional count per serving 32g total fat (10.2g saturated fat); 2424kJ (580 cal); 26.3g carbohydrate; 44.1g protein; 5.7g fibre

suitable to freeze at the end of step 3
lamb mixture can be marinaded overnight at the end of step 1.

GREEK-STYLE ROAST LAMB WITH POTATOES

prep + cook time 8 hours 40 minutes **serves** 4

2 tablespoons olive oil
1kg baby new potatoes
2kg leg of lamb
2 sprigs fresh rosemary,
chopped coarsely
2 tablespoons finely chopped
fresh flat-leaf parsley
2 tablespoons finely chopped
fresh oregano
3 cloves garlic, crushed
1 tablespoon finely grated
lemon rind
2 tablespoons lemon juice
½ cup (125ml) beef stock

1 Heat half the oil in large frying pan; cook potatoes until browned. Transfer to 4.5-litre slow cooker.
2 Make small cuts in lamb at 2.5cm intervals; press rosemary into cuts. Combine remaining oil, parsley, oregano, garlic, rind and juice in small bowl; rub mixture all over lamb, season.
3 Cook lamb in same heated pan until browned all over. Place lamb on top of potatoes; add stock. Cook, covered, on low, 8 hours.
4 Remove lamb and potatoes; cover lamb, stand 10 minutes before slicing.
5 Serve lamb with potatoes and sauce.

nutritional count per serving 29.5g total fat (10.2g saturated fat); 3206kJ (767 cal); 33.5g carbohydrate; 88.4g protein; 5.6g fibre

not suitable to freeze
lamb can be refrigerated, covered, overnight at the end of step 2

LAMB WITH QUINCE & HONEY

prep + cook time 8 hours 25 minutes (+ refrigeration) **serves** 4

1kg piece boneless lamb shoulder
6 cloves garlic, peeled, halved
2 tablespoons finely chopped
coriander roots and stems
2 teaspoons ground cumin
1 teaspoon ground coriander
1 teaspoon sweet paprika
2 tablespoons olive oil
1 medium brown onion (150g),
sliced thickly
1 cup (250ml) chicken stock
1 cinnamon stick
2 tablespoons honey
1 tablespoon quince paste
⅓ cup coarsely chopped fresh
coriander leaves

1 Roll and tie lamb with kitchen string at 5cm intervals. Using mortar and pestle, crush garlic, coriander roots and stems, spices and half the oil until almost smooth. Rub garlic mixture all over lamb; cover, refrigerate 2 hours.
2 Heat remaining oil in large frying pan; cook lamb, until browned all over. Remove from pan. Add onion to same pan; cook, stirring, until onion softens.
3 Place stock, cinnamon and onion mixture in 4.5-litre slow cooker; top with lamb, drizzle with honey. Season with salt and pepper. Cook, covered, on low, 8 hours. Stand lamb 10 minutes; stir quince paste into sauce.
4 Thickly slice lamb, serve with sauce; sprinkle with chopped coriander leaves. Serve lamb with couscous.

nutritional count per serving 31.5g total fat (11.4g saturated fat); 2366kJ (566 cal); 15.8g carbohydrate; 54g protein; 1.9g fibre

not suitable to freeze
lamb can be covered and refrigerated overnight at the end of step 1

RED CURRY LAMB SHANKS

prep + cook time 8 hours 40 minutes **serves** 6

2 tablespoons vegetable oil
6 french-trimmed lamb
shanks (2kg)
1 large sweet potato (500g),
chopped coarsely
3 fresh kaffir lime leaves,
shredded thinly
1 large brown onion (200g),
chopped finely
2 tablespoons red curry paste
1²/₃ cups (400ml) canned
coconut cream
2 cups (500ml) chicken stock
2 tablespoons fish sauce
375g green beans,
chopped coarsely
1 cup loosely packed fresh
coriander leaves
2 tablespoons lime juice

1 Heat half the oil in large frying pan; cook lamb, in batches, until browned all over. Place lamb in 4.5-litre slow cooker, add sweet potato and lime leaves.

2 Heat remaining oil in same pan; cook onion, stirring, until soft. Add curry paste; cook, stirring, until fragrant. Add coconut cream; bring to the boil. Remove pan from heat; stir in stock and sauce, pour over lamb. Cook, covered, on low, 8 hours.

3 Add green beans to cooker; cook, covered, on high, about 15 minutes. Stir in coriander and juice; season to taste. Serve with steamed rice.

nutritional count per serving 33.2g total fat (18g saturated fat); 2337kJ (559 cal); 17g carbohydrate; 45.6g protein; 6g fibre

suitable to freeze at the end of step 2

tip Red curry paste is available in various strengths from supermarkets. Use whichever one suits your spice-level tolerance best.

HONEY & BALSAMIC BRAISED PORK

prep + cook time 8 hours **serves** 6

2 tablespoons olive oil
1.2kg piece pork neck
9 shallots (225g), halved
1½ cups (375ml) chicken stock
⅓ cup (80ml) white
balsamic vinegar
¼ cup (90g) honey
6 cloves garlic, peeled
2 sprigs fresh rosemary
1 cup (160g) pitted green olives

1 Heat oil in large frying pan; cook pork until browned all over. Remove from pan.
2 Add shallots to same pan; cook, stirring, until browned all over. Add stock, vinegar and honey; bring to the boil.
3 Place garlic and rosemary in 4.5-litre slow cooker; top with pork. Pour over shallot mixture; cook, covered, on low, 7 hours.
4 Add olives; cook, covered, on low, 30 minutes. Season to taste.
5 Remove pork; stand, covered, 10 minutes before slicing. Serve pork drizzled with sauce.

nutritional count per serving 23.6g total fat (6.5g saturated fat); 1969kJ (471 cal); 20g carbohydrate; 44g protein; 1.1g fibre

suitable to freeze at the end of step 3

PORK NECK WITH CIDER & PEAR

prep + cook time 6½ hours **serves** 4

1kg piece pork neck
185g Italian pork sausages
1 egg yolk
½ cup (70g) coarsely
chopped pistachios
2 tablespoons coarsely
chopped fresh sage
1 tablespoon olive oil
1 medium brown onion
(150g), quartered
4 cloves garlic, halved
2 medium unpeeled pears
(460g), quartered
⅔ cup (160ml) apple cider
6 fresh sage leaves

1 Place pork on board; slice through thickest part of pork horizontally, without cutting all the way through. Open pork out to form one large piece; trim pork.

2 Squeeze filling from sausages into small bowl, mix in egg yolk, nuts and chopped sage; season. Press sausage mixture along one long side of pork; roll pork to enclose filling. Tie pork with kitchen string at 2.5cm intervals.

3 Heat oil in large frying pan; cook pork, until browned all over. Remove from pan. Add onion and garlic to same pan; cook, stirring, until onion softens.

4 Place pears and onion mixture in 4.5-litre slow cooker; top with pork then add cider and sage leaves. Cook, covered, on low, 6 hours.

5 Serve sliced pork with pear and onion mixture. Sprinkle with extra sage leaves, if you like.

nutritional count per serving 45.3g total fat (13g saturated fat); 3164kJ (757 cal); 19g carbohydrate; 63g protein; 5.6g fibre

not suitable to freeze.

tip Italian sausages are coarse pork sausages generally sold in plump links. They are usually flavoured with garlic and fennel seed or anise seed. Substitute any spicy pork sausages if you cannot obtain them.

CHAR SIU PORK RIBS

prep + cook time 7 hours 25 minutes **serves** 6

2.5kg pork spare rib racks
2 tablespoons groundnut oil
½ cup (125ml) char siu sauce
2 tablespoons light soy sauce
¼ cup (60ml) orange juice
5cm piece fresh ginger
(25g), grated
2 cloves garlic, crushed
1 fresh long red chilli,
chopped finely
2 teaspoons sesame oil

1 Cut rib racks into pieces to fit 4.5-litre slow cooker. Heat groundnut oil in large frying pan; cook ribs, in batches, until browned all over.
2 Meanwhile, combine sauces, juice, ginger, garlic, chilli and sesame oil in jug; brush all over ribs. Place ribs in cooker; pour over remaining sauce. Cook, covered, on low, 7 hours.
3 Remove ribs from sauce; cover to keep warm. Place sauce in medium saucepan; bring to the boil. Boil, uncovered, about 5 minutes or until sauce is thickened slightly.
4 Serve ribs drizzled with sauce.

nutritional count per serving 23.9g total fat (6.6g saturated fat); 1760kJ (421 cal); 9.6g carbohydrate; 40.7g protein; 2.7g fibre

not suitable to freeze

tip Ask the butcher to cut the rib racks into pieces that will fit your slow cooker. Char siu sauce is available online and at Chinese supermarkets.

SPICY TOMATO & SAFFRON CHICKEN CASSEROLE

prep + cook time 6 hours 25 minutes **serves** 6

¼ cup (35g) plain flour
2 tablespoons moroccan seasoning
6 chicken thighs (1.2kg)
1 tablespoon vegetable oil
1 large brown onion (200g), sliced thickly
2 cloves garlic, crushed
2.5cm piece fresh ginger (15g), grated
1 fresh long red chilli, sliced thinly
2 cups (500ml) chicken stock
400g canned chopped tomatoes
¼ cup (70g) tomato paste
¼ teaspoon saffron threads

preserved lemon gremolata
⅔ cup finely chopped fresh flat-leaf parsley
1 tablespoon thinly sliced preserved lemon rind
1 clove garlic, crushed

1 Combine flour and 1 tablespoon of the seasoning in small shallow bowl; toss chicken in flour mixture to coat, shake off excess. Heat half the oil in large frying pan; cook chicken, in batches, until browned. Transfer to 4.5-litre slow cooker.
2 Heat remaining oil in same pan, add onion, garlic, ginger, chilli and remaining seasoning; cook, stirring, until onion softens. Add ½ cup of the stock; cook, stirring, until mixture boils.
3 Stir onion mixture into cooker with remaining stock, undrained tomatoes, paste and saffron. Cook, covered, on low, 6 hours. Season to taste.
4 Make preserved lemon gremolata before serving.
5 Sprinkle casserole with gremolata. Serve with steamed rice or couscous.

preserved lemon gremolata Combine ingredients in small bowl.

nutritional count per serving 23.8g total fat (7.2g saturated fat); 1522kJ (364 cal); 10.2g carbohydrate; 26.5g protein; 2.5g fibre

suitable to freeze at the end of step 3

COQ AU VIN

prep + cook time 8 hours **serves** 6

20 spring onions (500g)
2 tablespoons olive oil
6 slices rindless bacon (390g),
sliced thinly
440g button mushrooms
2 cloves garlic, crushed
1.8kg whole chicken
2 cups (500ml) dry red wine
2 medium carrots (240g),
chopped coarsely
3 bay leaves
4 sprigs fresh thyme
2 sprigs fresh rosemary
1½ cups (375ml) chicken stock
¼ cup (70g) tomato paste
¼ cup (35g) cornflour
2 tablespoons water

1 Trim green ends from onions, leaving about 4cm of stem attached; trim roots leaving onions intact. Heat half the oil in large frying pan; cook onions, stirring, until browned all over, remove from pan. Add bacon, mushrooms and garlic to same pan; cook, stirring, until bacon is crisp, remove from pan.
2 Cut chicken into 12 pieces. Heat remaining oil in same pan; cook chicken, in batches, until browned all over; drain on absorbent paper. Add wine to same pan; bring to the boil, stirring.
3 Place chicken in 4.5-litre slow cooker with onions, bacon and mushroom mixture, carrot, herbs, stock, wine mixture and paste. Cook, covered, on low, 7 hours.
4 Stir in blended cornflour and the water; cook, covered, on high, about 20 minutes or until sauce thickens slightly. Season to taste.

nutritional count per serving 39.6g total fat (11.7g saturated fat); 2750kJ (658 cal); 12.3g carbohydrate; 47.8g protein; 5.1g fibre

not suitable to freeze

tip Use chicken pieces if you prefer, such as 6 thighs and 6 drumsticks or 6 leg portions, or ask your butcher to cut the whole chicken into 12 serving pieces for you.

GREEN OLIVE & LEMON CHICKEN

prep + cook time 6 hours 20 minutes **serves** 4

15g butter, softened
1 tablespoon olive oil
2 teaspoons finely grated
lemon rind
3 cloves garlic, crushed
¼ cup (30g) pitted green olives,
chopped finely
2 tablespoons finely chopped
fresh flat-leaf parsley
1.5kg whole chicken
2 unpeeled medium lemons
(280g), quartered

1 Combine butter, oil, rind, garlic, olives and parsley in medium bowl; season.
2 Rinse chicken under cold water; pat dry, inside and out, with absorbent paper. Use fingers to make a pocket between the breasts and skin; push half the butter mixture under skin. Rub remaining butter mixture all over chicken. Tuck wing tips under chicken; fill cavity with lemon, tie legs together with kitchen string. Trim skin around neck; secure neck flap to underside of chicken with small fine skewers.
3 Place chicken in 4.5-litre slow cooker. Cook, covered, on low, 6 hours.
4 Cut chicken into quarters to serve.

nutritional count per serving 38.1g total fat (12.1g saturated fat); 2086kJ (499 cal); 2g carbohydrate; 37.7g protein; 0.6g fibre

not suitable to freeze

BUTTER CHICKEN

prep + cook time 4½ hours (+ refrigeration) **serves** 6

12 chicken thighs (2.4kg), skin removed
2 tablespoons lemon juice
1 teaspoon chilli powder
¾ cup (200g) greek-style yogurt
5cm piece fresh ginger (25g), grated
2 teaspoons garam masala
45g butter
1 tablespoon vegetable oil
1 medium brown onion (150g), chopped finely
4 cloves garlic, crushed
1 teaspoon ground coriander
1 teaspoon ground cumin
1 teaspoon sweet paprika
2 tablespoons tomato paste
410g canned tomato purée
⅔ cup (160ml) chicken stock
2 tablespoons honey
1 cinnamon stick
⅓ cup (80ml) pouring cream
⅓ cup (80g) ricotta cheese
½ cup loosely packed fresh coriander leaves

1 Combine chicken, juice and chilli powder in large bowl. Cover, refrigerate 30 minutes.
2 Stir yogurt, ginger and half the garam masala into chicken mixture.
3 Heat butter and oil in large frying pan; cook chicken, in batches, until browned all over. Transfer chicken to 4.5-litre slow cooker. Add onion and garlic to same pan; cook, stirring, until onion softens. Add remaining garam masala and ground spices; cook, stirring, until fragrant. Remove from heat; stir in tomato paste, purée, stock, honey and cinnamon. Transfer tomato mixture to slow cooker. Cook, covered, on low, 4 hours.
4 Stir in cream; season to taste.
5 Serve topped with ricotta and coriander leaves and accompanied with steamed basmati rice and some warm naan bread.

nutritional count per serving 39.3g total fat (17g saturated fat); 2750kJ (658 cal); 17.9g carbohydrate; 57.8g protein; 2.6g fibre

suitable to freeze at the end of step 3

SPICED CHICKEN IN COCONUT SAUCE

prep + cook time 7¾ hours **serves** 6

1 tablespoon groundnut oil
3 chicken thighs (660g), halved
6 chicken drumsticks (900g)
2 medium brown onions (300g),
chopped coarsely
1 cup (250ml) chicken stock
400ml canned coconut milk
3 fresh kaffir lime leaves,
shredded thinly
315g green beans, chopped coarsely
12 fresh thai aubergines
(350g), halved
¼ cup loosely packed fresh
coriander leaves

spice paste
4 shallots (100g), quartered
2 cloves garlic, chopped coarsely
5cm piece fresh ginger (25g),
chopped coarsely
2 teaspoons ground cumin
2 teaspoons ground coriander
2 teaspoons ground turmeric
3 fresh small red thai chillies,
chopped coarsely
2 tablespoons fish sauce
2 tablespoons groundnut oil
2 tablespoons lime juice
1 tablespoon grated palm sugar

1 Make spice paste.
2 Heat half the oil in large frying pan; cook chicken, in batches, until browned all over, place in 4.5-litre slow cooker. Heat remaining oil in same pan; cook onion, stirring, until soft. Add spice paste; cook, stirring, until fragrant. Add stock; bring to the boil.
3 Remove from heat; stir in coconut milk and lime leaves, pour over chicken. Cook, covered, on low, 7 hours.
4 Add beans and aubergine, cook, covered, on high, about 20 minutes or until vegetables are tender. Season to taste; sprinkle with coriander.

spice paste Blend or process ingredients until mixture is smooth.

nutritional count per serving 41.9g total fat (19.4g saturated fat); 2508kJ (600 cal); 11.6g carbohydrate; 42.5g protein; 5.5g fibre

suitable to freeze at the end of step 3

tip Thai aubergines can be found at speciality shops and delis. If you can't find them, use baby aubergines instead.

DUCK VINDALOO

prep + cook time 6¾ hours serves 6

1.8kg whole duck
¼ cup (35g) plain flour
1 tablespoon groundnut oil
2 teaspoons cumin seeds
2 teaspoons fenugreek seeds
1 teaspoon ground coriander
1 teaspoon ground turmeric
teaspoon ground cardamom
4 fresh small red thai chillies, chopped coarsely
3 cloves garlic, quartered
2.5cm piece fresh ginger (15g), sliced thinly
⅓ cup (80ml) white vinegar
½ cup (125ml) chicken stock
1 medium red onion (170g), chopped finely
4 medium potatoes (800g), chopped coarsely
2 tablespoons chicken gravy powder
2 tablespoons water
½ cup loosely packed fresh coriander leaves

1 Rinse duck under cold water; pat dry. Cut duck into six serving-sized pieces. Toss duck in flour, shake off excess. Heat oil in large frying pan; cook duck, in batches, until browned. Transfer to 4.5-litre slow cooker.
2 Meanwhile, dry-fry spices in small frying pan until fragrant; cool. Blend or process spices, chilli, garlic, ginger and vinegar until smooth.
3 Stir spice mixture into cooker with stock, onion and potato. Cook, covered, on low, 6 hours. Season to taste.
4 Transfer duck and potato to serving plate. Skim excess fat from sauce. Stir combined gravy powder and the water into sauce in slow cooker. Cook, covered, on high, about 10 minutes or until the sauce thickens.
5 Drizzle sauce over duck; sprinkle with coriander.

nutritional count per serving 66.5g total fat (19.6g saturated fat); 3323kJ (795 cal); 22.7g carbohydrate; 26.7g protein; 3g fibre

not suitable to freeze

tip This is a mild vindaloo. If you like it hotter, add more fresh chillies when you make the paste.

RABBIT WITH SWEET POTATO & SAGE

prep + cook time 6 hours 20 minutes **serves** 6

1.5kg rabbit
12 baby brown onions (300g)
1 medium sweet potato (450g),
chopped coarsely
2 medium potatoes (400g),
chopped coarsely
1 cup (250ml) verjuice
1 cup (250ml) chicken stock
2 cloves garlic, sliced thinly
¼ cup loosely packed fresh
sage leaves

1 Cut rabbit into six serving-sized pieces. Peel onions, leaving root ends intact.
2 Combine rabbit, onion and remaining ingredients in 4.5-litre slow cooker; cook, covered, on low, 6 hours. Season to taste.
3 Serve rabbit and vegetables drizzled with broth and accompanied with and steamed green beans.

nutritional count per serving 4.6g total fat (1.7g saturated fat); 1112kJ (266 cal); 21.6g carbohydrate; 32.6g protein; 3g fibre

not suitable to freeze

tip Ask the butcher to cut the rabbit into pieces for you. Verjuice is available in delis and online. It's made from unripe grapes and has a slightly acidic taste.

ARTICHOKES WITH GARLIC ANCHOVY CRUMBS

prep + cook time 8 hours 35 minutes **serves** 6 (as a starter)

6 medium globe artichokes (1.2kg)
2 litres (8 cups) water
2 cups (500ml) chicken stock
2 tablespoons lemon juice
¼ cup (60ml) olive oil

garlic anchovy crumbs
1 tablespoon olive oil
6 anchovy fillets, drained,
chopped finely
3 cloves garlic, crushed
1½ cups (105g) stale breadcrumbs
1 tablespoon finely grated
lemon rind
⅓ cup finely chopped fresh
flat-leaf parsley
½ cup (40g) finely grated
pecorino cheese

1 Remove and discard tough outer leaves from artichokes. Trim stems so that artichoke bases sit flat. Using a small teaspoon, remove and discard hairy chokes from centre of artichokes; rinse artichokes under cold water.

2 Pack artichokes tightly, upside down, into 4.5-litre slow cooker; pour in the water, stock and juice. Cook, covered, on low, 8 hours.

3 Make garlic anchovy crumbs before serving.

4 Remove artichokes with slotted spoon; drain well. Serve artichokes with olive oil and garlic anchovy crumbs for dipping.

garlic anchovy crumbs Heat oil in large frying pan; cook anchovy and garlic, stirring, until anchovy softens. Add breadcrumbs and rind; cook, stirring, until crumbs are browned lightly and crisp. Transfer to medium bowl; cool. Stir in parsley and cheese; season to taste.

nutritional count per serving 6.2g total fat (1.8g saturated fat); 648kJ (155 cal); 13.9g carbohydrate; 9.5g protein; 2.3g fibre

not suitable to freeze

tip Serve with some crusty bread and a green or tomato salad to make a main meal.

RATATOUILLE

prep + cook time 4 hours 20 minutes **serves** 6

2 tablespoons olive oil
1 large red onion (300g),
chopped coarsely
3 cloves garlic, crushed
½ cup loosely packed fresh
basil leaves
2 tablespoons tomato paste
3 cups (700g) passata
2 teaspoons caster sugar
1 large aubergine (500g),
chopped coarsely
2 medium red pepper (400g),
chopped coarsely
2 large courgettes (300g),
chopped coarsely
1 medium green pepper (200g),
chopped coarsely

1 Heat oil in large frying pan; cook onion, garlic and half the basil, stirring, until onion softens. Add paste; cook, stirring, 1 minute. Remove from heat, stir in passata and sugar.
2 Place vegetables and sauce mixture into 4.5-litre slow cooker. Cook, covered, on low, 4 hours. Season to taste.
3 Serve ratatouille sprinkled with remaining basil.

nutritional count per serving 7.5g total fat (1g saturated fat); 803kJ (192 cal); 22.1g carbohydrate; 5.5g protein; 7g fibre

suitable to freeze at the end of step 2, although it's much better eaten straight after cooking

VANILLA & RED WINE POACHED PEARS

prep + cook time 4 hours 50 minutes (+ cooling) **serves** 6

6 medium firm pears (1.4kg)
2 cups (500ml) dry red wine
1½ cups (375ml) water
5cm piece orange rind
½ cup (125ml) orange juice
1 cup (220g) caster sugar
1 vanilla pod
1 cinnamon stick

1 Peel pears, leaving stems intact.
2 Combine wine, the water, rind, juice and sugar in 4.5-litre (18-cup) slow cooker. Halve vanilla pod lengthways, scrape seeds into slow cooker; add vanilla pod and cinnamon stick.
3 Lay pears down in cooker to cover in wine mixture. Cook, covered, on high, about 4½ hours or until pears are tender. Place 1 cup of the poaching liquid in small saucepan; bring to the boil. Boil, uncovered, about 7 minutes or until syrup is reduced by about half; cool.
4 Meanwhile, place pears in large deep bowl; add remaining poaching liquid, cool.
5 Serve pears drizzled with syrup.

nutritional count per serving 0.2g total fat (0g saturated fat); 1225kJ (293 cal); 55.9g carbohydrate; 0.8g protein; 3.3g fibre

not suitable to freeze

tip Store leftover poaching liquid in refrigerator for up to 1 month. Use for poaching more pears or stone fruit.

NUTTY BAKED APPLES WITH BUTTERSCOTCH SAUCE

prep + cook time 3 hours 20 minutes **serves** 6

6 small apples (780g)
90g butter, chopped finely
¼ cup (35g) slivered almonds
¼ cup (30g) finely chopped walnuts
½ teaspoon ground cinnamon
1 cup (220g) firmly packed light brown sugar
¾ cup (180ml) pouring cream
½ cup (125ml) apple juice

1 Core unpeeled apples about three-quarters of the way through, making hole 4cm in diameter. Use small sharp knife to score around centre of each apple.

2 Combine one-third of the butter with nuts, cinnamon and ¼ cup of the sugar in small bowl. Press mixture into apple cavities.

3 Combine cream, juice, remaining butter and sugar in 4.5-litre slow cooker. Stand apples upright in sauce. Cook, covered, on high, about 2½ hours, turning apples once, or until apples are tender.

4 Remove apples from cooker; cover to keep warm. Drain sauce into small saucepan; bring to the boil. Boil, uncovered, about 5 minutes or until sauce is thickened slightly.

5 Serve apples drizzled with sauce.

nutritional count per serving 32.1g total fat (17.1g saturated fat); 2107kJ (504 cal); 50.1g carbohydrate; 2.9g protein; 2.8g fibre

not suitable to freeze

tip Make sure the apples don't touch the side of the slow cooker.

CHOCOLATE SELF-SAUCING PUDDING

prep + cook time 2 hours 50 minutes **serves** 6

90g butter
¾ cup (180ml) milk
1 teaspoon vanilla extract
1 cup (220g) caster sugar
1½ cups (225g) self-raising flour
2 tablespoons cocoa powder
1 egg, beaten lightly
1 cup (220g) firmly packed light brown sugar
2 tablespoons cocoa powder, extra
2½ cups (625ml) boiling water

1 Grease 4.5-litre slow cooker bowl.

2 Melt butter in milk over low heat in medium saucepan. Remove from heat; cool 5 minutes. Stir in extract and caster sugar, then sifted flour and cocoa, and egg. Spread mixture into cooker bowl.

3 Sift brown sugar and extra cocoa evenly over mixture; gently pour boiling water evenly over mixture. Cook, covered, on high, about 2½ hours or until centre is firm.

4 Remove bowl from cooker. Stand pudding 5 minutes before serving. Serve pudding, hot or warm, dusted with a little sifted icing sugar, and with cream and/or ice-cream.

nutritional count per serving 15.5g total fat (9.6g saturated fat); 2424kJ (580 cal); 101.3g carbohydrate; 6.9g protein; 1.6g fibre

not suitable to freeze

MANDARIN & ALMOND PUDDING

prep + cook time 5½ hours **serves** 8

4 small mandarins (400g)
4 eggs
⅔ cup (150g) caster sugar
1⅓ cups (160g) ground almonds
⅔ cup (100g) self-raising flour

1 Place washed unpeeled mandarins in 4.5-litre slow cooker; cover with hot water. Cook, covered, on high, 2 hours.
2 Trim ends from mandarins; discard. Halve mandarins; remove and discard seeds. Process mandarins, including rind, until mixture is pulpy.
3 Grease 2-litre pudding basin.
4 Beat eggs and sugar in small bowl with electric mixer until thick and creamy; fold in ground almonds, sifted flour and mandarin pulp. Spoon mixture into basin. Top with pleated baking parchment and foil; secure with kitchen string or lid.
5 Place pudding in cooker with enough boiling water to come halfway up side of basin. Cook, covered, on high, 3 hours, replenishing with boiling water as necessary to maintain level. Stand pudding 5 minutes before turning onto plate. Serve pudding with cream, custard or ice-cream.

nutritional count per serving 13.9g total fat (1.6g saturated fat); 1246kJ (298 cal); 32.5g carbohydrate; 9g protein; 3.2g fibre

not suitable to freeze

tip The pleated paper and foil simply allow space for the pudding mixture to rise.

on the hob

CREAMY CHICKPEA & GARLIC SOUP

prep + cook time 2½ hours (+ standing) **serves** 4

2 cups (400g) dried chickpeas
1 tablespoon olive oil
1 large brown onion (200g),
chopped coarsely
4 cloves garlic, crushed
1.75 litres (7 cups) water
2 bay leaves
1 sprig fresh rosemary
300ml pouring cream

1 Place chickpeas in large bowl, cover with water; stand overnight, drain. Rinse under cold water, drain.
2 Heat oil in large saucepan; cook onion and garlic, stirring, until onion softens. Add chickpeas, the water, bay leaves and rosemary; bring to the boil. Reduce heat; simmer, covered, about 2 hours or until chickpeas are tender.
3 Remove from heat; cool 10 minutes. Discard bay leaves and rosemary.
4 Using hand-held blender, process soup in pan until smooth. Add cream; stir over medium heat until hot.

nutritional count per serving 39.9g total fat (22.5g saturated fat); 2048kJ (490 cal); 21.1g carbohydrate; 10g protein; 6.9g fibre

slow cooker: suitable to the end of step 2
suitable to freeze at the end of step 2

HEARTY WINTER SOUP

prep + cook time 2½ hours **serves** 4

2 tablespoons olive oil
1kg stewing beef, trimmed, cut into 2cm pieces
12 shallots (300g), halved
2 cloves garlic, crushed
2 small parsnips (240g), chopped coarsely
2 small turnips (300g), chopped coarsely
2 medium swedes (450g), chopped coarsely
300g piece butternut squash, chopped coarsely
1 cup (250ml) dry white wine
3 cups (750ml) beef stock
3 cups (750ml) water
1 tablespoon tomato paste
4 sprigs fresh thyme
⅓ cup short-cut vermicelli noodles

1 Heat half the oil in large saucepan; cook beef, in batches, until browned. Remove from pan.

2 Heat remaining oil in same pan; cook shallot and garlic, stirring, until shallot softens.

3 Add vegetables, wine, stock, the water, paste and thyme to pan; bring to the boil. Reduce heat; simmer, covered, 1½ hours, stirring occasionally.

4 Add noodles to pan; cook, uncovered, about 10 minutes or until just softened.

nutritional count per serving 21.4g total fat (6.5g saturated fat); 2387kJ (571 cal); 22g carbohydrate; 58.5g protein; 7.6g fibre

slow cooker: suitable to the end of step 3
suitable to freeze at the end of step 3

INDIAN DRY BEEF CURRY

prep + cook time 2 hours **serves** 6

2 tablespoons groundnut oil
2 medium brown onions (300g), chopped coarsely
4 cloves garlic, crushed
4cm piece fresh ginger (20g), grated
2 teaspoons ground cumin
2 teaspoons ground coriander
2 teaspoons ground garam masala
1 teaspoon ground turmeric
1.5kg braising steak, cut into 2cm pieces
1 cup (250ml) beef stock
½ cup (140g) natural yogurt
¼ cup loosely packed fresh coriander leaves

1 Heat oil in large saucepan; cook onion, garlic, ginger and spices, stirring occasionally, until onion softens. Add beef; cook, stirring, until beef is covered in spice mixture.
2 Add stock to pan; bring to the boil. Reduce heat; simmer, covered, 1 hour, stirring occasionally.
3 Uncover; cook, stirring occasionally, about 30 minutes or until liquid has almost evaporated and beef is tender.
4 Serve curry topped with yogurt and sprinkled with coriander.

nutritional count per serving 18.3g total fat (6.4g saturated fat); 1659kJ (397 cal); 4.5g carbohydrate; 53g protein; 1.1g fibre

slow cooker: suitable to the end of step 2
suitable to freeze at the end of step 3

PROVENÇALE BEEF CASSEROLE

prep + cook time 2½ hours **serves** 4

2 tablespoons olive oil
1kg stewing beef, cut into
2cm pieces
2 rindless bacon slices (130g),
chopped finely
1 medium leek (350g), sliced thinly
2 medium carrots (240g),
chopped coarsely
1 stalk celery (150g), trimmed,
chopped coarsely
2 cloves garlic, crushed
410g canned tomatoes, crushed
1½ cups (375ml) beef stock
1 cup (250ml) dry red wine
2 bay leaves
4 sprigs fresh thyme
6 sprigs fresh flat-leaf parsley
2 medium courgettes (240g),
sliced thickly
½ cup (75g) pitted black olives

1 Heat oil in large saucepan; cook beef, in batches, until browned. Remove from pan.

2 Cook bacon, leek, carrot, celery and garlic, in same heated pan, stirring, until leek softens.

3 Return beef to pan with undrained tomatoes, stock, wine, bay leaves, thyme and parsley; bring to the boil. Reduce heat; simmer, covered, 1 hour, stirring occasionally.

4 Add courgettes and olives to pan; simmer, covered, 30 minutes or until beef is tender.

5 Remove and discard bay leaves, thyme and parsley before serving.

nutritional count per serving 25.8g total fat (7.8g saturated fat); 2458kJ (588 cal); 14.1g carbohydrate; 61.4g protein; 6.4g fibre

slow cooker: suitable to the end of step 3
suitable to freeze at the end of step 3

MEXICAN BEANS WITH SAUSAGES

prep + cook time 2½ hours (+ standing) **serves** 4

1 cup (200g) dried kidney beans
750g beef sausages,
chopped coarsely
1 tablespoon olive oil
1 large white onion (200g),
chopped coarsely
3 cloves garlic, crushed
1 large red pepper (350g),
chopped coarsely
½ teaspoon ground cumin
2 teaspoons sweet smoked paprika
1 teaspoon dried chilli flakes
800g canned tomatoes, crushed
2 tablespoons coarsely
chopped fresh oregano

1 Place beans in medium bowl, cover with cold water; stand overnight, drain. Rinse under cold water; drain. Place beans in medium saucepan of boiling water; return to the boil. Reduce heat; simmer, uncovered, about 30 minutes or until beans are almost tender. Drain.

2 Cook sausages, in batches, in heated large deep saucepan until browned; drain on absorbent paper.

3 Heat oil in same pan; cook onion, garlic and pepper, stirring, until onion softens. Add cumin, paprika and chilli; cook, stirring, about 2 minutes or until fragrant. Add beans and undrained tomatoes; bring to the boil. Reduce heat; simmer, covered, about 1 hour or until beans are tender.

4 Return sausages to pan; simmer, covered, about 10 minutes or until sausages are cooked through. Remove from heat; stir in oregano.

nutritional count per serving 56.9g total fat (25.2g saturated fat); 3323kJ (795 cal); 33.5g carbohydrate; 38.1g protein; 20.2g fibre

slow cooker: not suitable
suitable to freeze at the end of step 4

NAVARIN OF LAMB

prep + cook time 2 hours **serves** 4

2 tablespoons olive oil
8 lamb noisettes (800g)
1 large brown onion (200g), sliced thickly
2 cloves garlic, crushed
2 tablespoons plain flour
1 cup (250ml) water
3 cups (750ml) chicken stock
½ cup (125ml) dry red wine
400g canned chopped tomatoes
¼ cup (70g) tomato paste
2 bay leaves
2 sprigs fresh rosemary
2 stalks celery (300g), trimmed, cut into 5cm lengths
150g green beans, trimmed, halved
20 baby carrots (400g), trimmed
200g button mushrooms
1 cup (120g) frozen peas
½ cup coarsely chopped fresh flat-leaf parsley

1 Heat oil in large saucepan; cook lamb, in batches, until browned. Remove from pan. Cook onion and garlic in same heated pan, stirring, until onion softens. Add flour; cook, stirring, until mixture bubbles and thickens. Gradually add the water, stock and wine; stir until mixture boils and thickens.

2 Return lamb to pan with undrained tomatoes, paste, bay leaves and rosemary; bring to the boil. Reduce heat; simmer, covered, 30 minutes.

3 Add celery, beans, carrots and mushrooms to pan; simmer, covered, about 30 minutes or until vegetables are tender. Add peas; simmer, uncovered, until peas are just tender.

4 Remove and discard toothpicks from lamb. Serve sprinkled with parsley.

nutritional count per serving 32.6g total fat (12.9g saturated fat); 2913kJ (697 cal); 21.4g carbohydrate; 69.3g protein; 11g fibre

slow cooker: not suitable
not suitable to freeze

tip Lamb noisettes are boned and rolled lamb loin chops that are usually secured with toothpicks (remove before serving).

IRISH LAMB & BARLEY STEW

prep + cook time 2 hours **serves** 4

2 tablespoons olive oil
1kg diced lamb shoulder
1 large brown onion (200g), chopped coarsely
2 medium carrots (240g), chopped coarsely
2 stalks celery (300g), trimmed, chopped coarsely
2 cloves garlic, crushed
1 litre (4 cups) chicken stock
2 cups (500ml) water
1 cup (200g) pearl barley
4 sprigs fresh thyme
3 medium potatoes (600g), chopped coarsely
2 cups (160g) finely shredded cabbage
⅓ cup finely chopped fresh flat-leaf parsley

1 Heat half the oil in large saucepan; cook lamb, in batches, until browned. Remove from pan.

2 Heat remaining oil in same pan; cook onion, carrot, celery and garlic, stirring, until vegetables soften. Return lamb to pan with stock, the water, barley and thyme; bring to the boil. Reduce heat; simmer, covered, 1 hour, skimming fat from surface occasionally.

3 Add potato; simmer, uncovered, about 20 minutes or until potato is tender.

4 Add cabbage; simmer, uncovered, until cabbage is just tender. Discard thyme.

5 Serve stew sprinkled with parsley.

nutritional count per serving 22.6g total fat (8.2g saturated fat); 2224kJ (532 cal); 37.4g carbohydrate; 40.4g protein; 8.6g fibre

slow cooker: suitable to the end of step 2
suitable to freeze at the end of step 2

ROGAN JOSH

prep + cook time 2½ hours serves 4

2 teaspoons ground cardamom
2 teaspoons ground cumin
2 teaspoons ground coriander
1kg boned leg of lamb, trimmed,
cut into 3cm pieces
20g butter
2 tablespoons vegetable oil
2 medium brown onions (300g),
sliced thinly
4cm piece fresh ginger
(20g), grated
4 cloves garlic, crushed
2 teaspoons sweet paprika
½ teaspoon cayenne pepper
½ cup (125ml) beef stock
425g canned tomatoes, crushed
2 bay leaves
2 cinnamon sticks
¾ cup (200g) yogurt
¾ cup (110g) roasted slivered
almonds
1 fresh long red chilli, sliced thinly

cucumber raita
1 cup (280g) greek-style
natural yogurt
½ cucumber (130g) deseeded,
chopped finely
1 tablespoon finely chopped
fresh mint

1 Combine cardamom, cumin and coriander in medium bowl, add lamb; toss lamb to coat in spice mixture.
2 Heat butter and half the oil in large deep saucepan; cook lamb, in batches, until browned all over. Remove from pan.
3 Heat remaining oil in same pan; cook onion, ginger, garlic, paprika and cayenne over low heat, stirring, until onion softens.
4 Return lamb to pan with stock, undrained tomatoes, bay leaves and cinnamon. Add yogurt, 1 tablespoon at a time, stirring well between each addition; bring to the boil. Reduce heat; simmer, covered, about 1½ hours or until lamb is tender.
5 Meanwhile, make cucumber raita.
6 Sprinkle lamb with nuts and chilli off the heat; serve with raita.

cucumber raita Combine ingredients in small bowl. Season with salt, pepper and ground cumin to taste.

nutritional count per serving 48.1g total fat (15.3g saturated fat); 3219kJ (770 cal); 15.7g carbohydrate; 68.9g protein; 5.5g fibre

slow cooker: not suitable
not suitable to freeze

MAPLE SYRUP-GLAZED LAMB SHANKS

prep + cook time 2¼ hours **serves** 4

⅓ cup (80ml) maple syrup
1 cup (250ml) chicken stock
1 tablespoon dijon mustard
1 cups (375ml) orange juice
8 lamb shanks (2kg)

roast potatoes
3 medium potatoes (600g), halved
2 tablespoons olive oil

1 Combine syrup, stock, mustard and juice in large deep flameproof casserole dish, add lamb; toss lamb to coat in syrup mixture. Bring to the boil, then cover tightly. Reduce heat; cook lamb, turning every 20 minutes, about 2 hours or until lamb is tender.
2 Make roast potatoes; serve with lamb shanks and just-wilted baby spinach leaves.

roast potatoes Preheat oven to 220°C/200°C fan-assisted. Lightly oil oven tray. Boil, steam or microwave potatoes 5 minutes; drain. Pat dry with absorbent paper; cool 10 minutes. Gently rake rounded sides of potatoes with tines of fork; place potato, in single layer, cut-side down, on oven tray. Brush with oil; roast, uncovered, in oven, about 50 minutes or until browned lightly and crisp.

nutritional count per serving 34.2g total fat (12.7g saturated fat); 3089kJ (738 cal); 45.5g carbohydrate; 60.7g protein; 2.7g fibre

slow cooker: suitable to the end of step 1
suitable to freeze at the end of step 1

DRUNKEN DUCK

prep + cook time 2¾ hours **serves** 4

2kg whole duck
1 tablespoon vegetable oil
1 medium brown onion (150g),
chopped coarsely
2 cloves garlic, crushed
1 fresh small red thai chilli,
chopped finely
4cm piece fresh ginger
(20g), grated
2 cups (500ml) chinese
cooking wine
1 cup (250ml) water
1 tablespoon dark soy sauce
½ teaspoon five-spice powder
15g dried shiitake
mushrooms, halved
4 spring onions, sliced thinly

1 Discard neck from duck. Rinse duck under cold water; pat dry inside and out with absorbent paper. Heat oil in large saucepan; cook duck until browned all over. Remove from pan.
2 Reserve 1 tablespoon of the pan drippings; discard the remainder. Heat reserved drippings in pan, add brown onion, garlic, chilli and ginger; cook, stirring, until onion softens. Return duck to pan with cooking wine, the water, sauce, five-spice and mushrooms; bring to the boil. Simmer, covered, 2 hours, turning duck occasionally.
3 Carefully remove duck from pan; cut into four pieces. Divide duck among serving plates; drizzle with pan liquid, sprinkle with spring onion.

nutritional count per serving 20.5g total fat (6g saturated fat); 953kJ (228 cal); 1.2g carbohydrate; 7.2g protein; 0.2g fibre

slow cooker: not suitable
not suitable to freeze

in the oven

BRAISED BEEF CHEEKS IN RED WINE

prep + cooking time 4 hours **serves** 4

2 tablespoons olive oil
1.6kg beef cheeks, trimmed
1 medium brown onion (150g), chopped coarsely
1 medium carrot (120g), chopped coarsely
3 cups (750ml) dry red wine
¼ cup (60ml) red wine vinegar
800g canned whole tomatoes
¼ cup (55g) firmly packed light brown sugar
2 sprigs fresh rosemary
6 black peppercorns
2 tablespoons fresh oregano leaves
1 large fennel bulb (550g), cut into thin wedges
400g spring onions, trimmed, halved
200g chestnut mushrooms

cheesy polenta
2⅓ cups (580ml) water
2⅓ cups (580ml) milk
1 cup (340g) polenta
½ cup (20g) finely grated parmesan cheese
30g butter

1 Preheat oven to 160°C/140°C fan-assisted.
2 Heat half the oil in large flameproof casserole dish on hob; cook beef, in batches, until browned all over. Remove from dish.
3 Heat remaining oil in same dish; cook brown onion and carrot, stirring, until onion softens. Return beef to dish with wine, vinegar, undrained tomatoes, sugar, rosemary, peppercorns, oregano and fennel; bring to the boil. Cover, transfer to oven; cook 2 hours.
4 Stir in spring onion and mushrooms; cook, uncovered, in oven, about 45 minutes or until beef is tender.
5 Meanwhile, make cheesy polenta; serve with beef.

cheesy polenta Combine water and milk in large saucepan; bring to the boil. Gradually add polenta to liquid, stirring constantly. Reduce heat; simmer, stirring, about 10 minutes or until polenta thickens. Stir in cheese and butter.

nutritional count per serving 56.7g total fat (24g saturated fat); 6069kJ (1452 cal); 95g carbohydrate; 103.6g protein; 11.3g fibre

slow cooker: suitable to the end of step 3
suitable to freeze at the end of step 3

BEEF STEW WITH PARSLEY DUMPLINGS

prep + cook time 3 hours **serves** 4

1kg beef braising steak, diced into 5cm pieces
2 tablespoons plain flour
2 tablespoons olive oil
20g butter
2 medium brown onions (300g), chopped coarsely
2 cloves garlic, crushed
2 medium carrots (240g), chopped coarsely
1 cup (250ml) dry red wine
2 tablespoons tomato paste
2 cups (500ml) beef stock
4 sprigs fresh thyme

parsley dumplings
1 cup (150g) self-raising flour
50g butter
1 egg, beaten lightly
¼ cup (20g) coarsely grated parmesan cheese
¼ cup finely chopped fresh flat-leaf parsley
⅓ cup (50g) drained sun-dried tomatoes, chopped finely
¼ cup (60ml) milk, approximately

1 Preheat oven to 160°C/140°C fan-assisted.

2 Coat beef in flour; shake off excess. Heat oil in large flameproof casserole dish on the hob; cook beef, in batches, until browned all over. Remove from dish.

3 Melt butter in same heated dish; cook onion, garlic and carrot, stirring, until vegetables soften. Add wine; cook, stirring, until liquid reduces to ¼ cup. Return beef to dish with paste, stock and thyme; bring to the boil. Cover, transfer to oven; cook 1¾ hours.

4 Meanwhile, make parsley dumpling mixture.

5 Remove dish from oven; drop level tablespoons of the dumpling mixture, about 2cm apart, onto top of stew. Cook, uncovered, in oven, about 20 minutes or until dumplings are browned lightly and cooked through. Serve stew with a mixed green leafy salad dressed with a vinaigrette.

parsley dumplings Place flour in medium bowl; rub in butter. Stir in egg, cheese, parsley, tomato and enough milk to make a soft, sticky dough.

nutritional count per serving 39.7g total fat (17.4g saturated fat); 3457kJ (827 cal); 43g carbohydrate; 63.9g protein; 6.7g fibre

slow cooker: suitable to the end of step 3
suitable to freeze at the end of step 3

VEAL WITH ARTICHOKES, OLIVES & LEMON

prep + cook time 3 hours **serves** 6

1 medium unpeeled lemon (140g),
chopped coarsely
4 medium globe artichokes (800g)
1.2kg diced veal neck
¼ cup (35g) plain flour
50g butter
¼ cup (60ml) olive oil
1 medium brown onion (150g),
chopped finely
1 medium carrot (120g),
chopped finely
2 cloves garlic, chopped finely
2 sprigs fresh marjoram
2 sprigs fresh oregano
1 cup (250ml) dry white wine
2 cups (500ml) chicken stock
1 cup (150g) pitted kalamata olives
2 teaspoons finely grated
lemon rind
2 tablespoons lemon juice
2 tablespoons fresh oregano leaves
1 medium lemon (140g),
cut into wedges

1 Place chopped lemon in large bowl half-filled with cold water. Discard outer leaves from artichokes; cut tips from remaining leaves. Trim then peel stalks. Quarter artichokes lengthways; using teaspoon, remove and discard chokes. Place artichokes into the lemon water.
2 Preheat oven to 160°C/140°C fan-assisted.
3 Coat veal in flour; shake off excess. Heat butter and 2 tablespoons of the oil in large flameproof casserole dish on hob; cook veal, in batches, until browned. Remove from dish.
4 Heat remaining oil in same dish; cook onion, carrot, garlic, marjoram and oregano sprigs, stirring, until vegetables soften. Add wine; bring to the boil. Return veal to dish with stock; cover. Transfer to oven; cook 1 hour.
5 Add artichokes, cover; return to oven, cook 30 minutes. Uncover; cook about 30 minutes or until veal is tender.
6 Stir in olives, rind and juice. Divide among serving plates; top with oregano leaves. Serve with lemon wedges and penne pasta.

nutritional count per serving 21.6g total fat (7.4g saturated fat); 2040kJ (488 cal); 14.6g carbohydrate; 50.2g protein; 3.4g fibre

slow cooker: suitable to the end of step 5
suitable to freeze at the end of step 4

ANCHOVY & CHILLI LAMB NECK CHOPS WITH CREAMY POLENTA

prep + cook time 3 hours (+ refrigeration) **serves** 4

4 drained anchovy fillets, chopped finely
2 fresh small red thai chillies, chopped finely
4 cloves garlic, crushed
½ cup (125ml) dry red wine
8 lamb neck chops (1.4kg), trimmed
2 tablespoons olive oil
1 medium brown onion (150g), chopped coarsely
1 tablespoon plain flour
400g canned tomatoes, crushed
2 cups (500ml) beef stock

creamy polenta
2 cups (500ml) milk
2 cups (500ml) water
1 cup (170g) polenta
½ cup (40g) finely grated parmesan cheese
½ cup (125ml) pouring cream
½ cup coarsely chopped fresh flat-leaf parsley

1 Combine anchovy, chilli, garlic and wine in medium bowl, add lamb; turn lamb to coat in marinade. Cover; refrigerate 3 hours or overnight.

2 Preheat oven to 160°C/140°C fan-assisted.

3 Heat half the oil in deep medium baking dish on stove top; cook undrained lamb, in batches, until browned all over. Remove from dish. Heat remaining oil in same dish; cook onion, stirring, until softened. Add flour; cook, stirring, about 5 minutes or until flour mixture browns lightly.

4 Return lamb to dish with undrained tomatoes and stock; cover. Transfer to oven; cook 1½ hours.

5 Uncover, skim fat from surface, return to oven; cook, uncovered, turning lamb occasionally, about 30 minutes or until lamb is tender.

6 Meanwhile, make creamy polenta.

7 Divide polenta among serving plates, top with lamb; sprinkle with extra flat-leaf parsley to serve.

creamy polenta Combine milk and water in large saucepan; bring to the boil. Gradually add polenta to liquid, stirring constantly. Reduce heat; simmer, stirring, about 5 minutes or until polenta thickens. Stir in cheese, cream and parsley.

nutritional count per serving 43.1g total fat (19.4g saturated fat); 3791kJ (907 cal); 45g carbohydrate; 79.9g protein; 3.9g fibre

slow cooker: suitable to the end of step 5
suitable to freeze at the end of step 5

LAMB SHANKS BOURGUIGNON

prep + cook time 2½ hours **serves** 4

12 baby onions (300g)
8 french-trimmed lamb
shanks (2kg)
¼ cup (35g) plain flour
1 tablespoon olive oil
20g butter
6 slices rindless bacon (390g),
chopped coarsely
300g button mushrooms
2 cloves garlic, crushed
1 cup (250ml) dry red wine
1 cup (250ml) beef stock
1 cup (250ml) water
2 tablespoons tomato paste
2 bay leaves
1 tablespoon light brown sugar

1 Preheat oven to 200°C/180°C fan-assisted.

2 Peel onions, leaving root ends intact.

3 Coat lamb in flour; shake off excess. Heat oil in large flame-proof casserole dish on stove top; cook lamb, in batches, until browned. Remove from dish.

4 Melt butter in same heated dish; cook onions, bacon, mushrooms and garlic, stirring, until vegetables are browned lightly.

5 Return lamb to dish with wine, stock, the water, paste, bay leaves and sugar; bring to the boil. Cover dish; transfer to oven. Cook 1½ hours.

6 Uncover; cook in oven about 30 minutes or until lamb is tender and sauce thickens slightly.

7 Divide lamb among serving bowls; drizzle with sauce.

nutritional count per serving 37.5g total fat (15.2g saturated fat); 3248kJ (777 cal); 15.5g carbohydrate; 82.3g protein; 3.8g fibre

slow cooker: suitable to the end of step 6
not suitable to freeze.

BRAISED LEG OF LAMB WITH BEANS

prep + cook time 2½ hours (+ standing) **serves** 6

1 cup (200g) dried borlotti beans
6 cloves garlic, crushed
1 tablespoon coarsely chopped
fresh rosemary
2 teaspoons sea salt
1 teaspoon cracked black pepper
¼ cup (60ml) olive oil
1.5kg butterflied leg of lamb
2 medium brown onions (300g),
chopped coarsely
2 medium carrots (240g),
chopped coarsely
2 stalks celery (300g), trimmed,
chopped coarsely
2 bay leaves
2 sprigs fresh rosemary
1 cup (250ml) dry white wine
2 cups (500ml) chicken stock

mashed potatoes
4 medium potatoes (800g),
chopped coarsely
50g softened butter
½ cup (125ml) hot pouring cream

1 Place beans in medium bowl, cover with cold water; stand overnight, drain. Rinse under cold water; drain. Cook beans in medium saucepan of boiling water, uncovered, about 15 minutes or until beans are just tender; drain.
2 Preheat oven to 160°C/140°C fan-assisted
3 Combine garlic, chopped rosemary, salt, pepper and 1 tablespoon of the oil in small bowl. Place lamb, cut-side up, on board; rub garlic mixture into lamb. Roll lamb tightly; secure at 2cm intervals with kitchen string.
4 Heat remaining oil in large deep flameproof baking dish on hob; cook lamb until browned all over. Remove from dish.
5 Cook onion, carrot and celery in same heated dish, stirring, until onion softens. Add beans, bay leaves, rosemary sprigs, wine and stock to dish; bring to the boil.
6 Return lamb to dish, cover; transfer to oven, cook 1 hour.
7 Uncover; cook in oven 30 minutes. Discard herbs; remove lamb from dish. Cover; stand 10 minutes, then slice thickly.
8 Meanwhile, make mashed potatoes. Serve lamb on vegetable mixture, accompanied with mashed potatoes.

mashed potatoes Boil or steam potatoes until tender; drain. Mash potato with butter and cream until smooth.

nutritional count per serving 35.8g total fat (16.4g saturated fat); 2872kJ (687 cal); 32.2g carbohydrate; 49.6g protein; 6.2g fibre

slow cooker: suitable to the end of step 6
suitable to freeze at the end of step 7

ITALIAN BRAISED PORK

prep + cook time 3¼ hours **serves** 6

2 tablespoons olive oil
1.5kg pork shoulder, rolled and tied
2 cloves garlic, crushed
1 medium brown onion (150g), chopped coarsely
½ small fennel bulb (100g), chopped coarsely
8 slices pancetta (120g), chopped coarsely
1 tablespoon tomato paste
½ cup (125ml) dry white wine
400g canned whole tomatoes
1 cup (250ml) chicken stock
1 cup (250ml) water
2 sprigs fresh rosemary
2 large fennel bulbs (1kg), halved, sliced thickly

spice rub
1 teaspoon fennel seeds
2 teaspoons dried oregano
½ teaspoon cayenne pepper
1 tablespoon cracked black pepper
1 tablespoon sea salt
2 teaspoons olive oil

1 Preheat oven to 180°C/160°C fan-assisted.

2 Heat oil in large flameproof casserole dish on hob; cook pork until browned all over.

3 Meanwhile, combine ingredients for spice rub.

4 Remove pork from dish; discard all but 1 tablespoon of the oil in dish. Cook garlic, onion, chopped fennel and pancetta in same heated dish, stirring, until onion softens. Add paste; cook, stirring, 2 minutes.

5 Meanwhile, rub pork with spice rub.

6 Return pork to dish with wine, undrained tomatoes, stock, the water and rosemary; bring to the boil. Cover, transfer to oven; cook 1 hour.

7 Add sliced fennel to dish; cook, covered, in oven 1 hour. Remove pork from dish; discard rind. Cover pork to keep warm.

8 Meanwhile, cook braising liquid in dish over medium heat on stove top, uncovered, until thickened slightly. Return sliced pork to dish; serve pork with sauce.

nutritional count per serving 32.8g total fat (10.7g saturated fat); 2525kJ (604 cal); 7.5g carbohydrate; 66.5g protein; 4.6g fibre

slow cooker: suitable to the end of step 7
suitable to freeze at the end of step 6

tip Ask your butcher to roll and tie the pork shoulder for you.

CHICKEN & MERGUEZ CASSOULET

prep + cook time 3¼ hours (+ standing) **serves** 4

1½ cups (290g) dried butter beans
1 tablespoon vegetable oil
8 chicken thighs (1.3kg), halved
6 merguez sausages (480g)
1 large brown onion (200g),
chopped coarsely
2 medium carrots (240g),
cut into 1cm pieces
2 cloves garlic, chopped finely
4 sprigs fresh thyme
2 tablespoons tomato paste
1 teaspoon finely grated
lemon rind
425g canned chopped tomatoes
1 cup (250ml) chicken stock
1 cup (250ml) water
2 cups (140g) fresh breadcrumbs

spring onion couscous
2 cups (500ml) chicken stock
2 cups (400g) couscous
30g butter
2 spring onions, sliced thinly

1 Place beans in medium bowl, cover with cold water; stand overnight, drain. Rinse under cold water; drain. Cook beans in large saucepan of boiling water, uncovered, 10 minutes; drain.
2 Heat oil in large flameproof casserole dish on hob; cook chicken, in batches, until browned all over. Remove from dish. Cook sausages, in batches, in same heated dish until browned all over. Drain on absorbent paper; halve sausages. Reserve 1 tablespoon of fat from dish; discard remainder.
3 Preheat oven to 160°C/140°C fan-assisted.
4 Heat reserved fat in same dish on hob; cook onion, carrot, garlic and thyme, stirring, until onion softens. Add paste; cook, stirring, 2 minutes. Return chicken to dish with drained beans, rind, undrained tomatoes, stock and the water; bring to the boil. Cover, transfer to oven; cook 40 minutes.
5 Uncover; cook, in oven, about 1¼ hours or until liquid is almost absorbed and beans are tender.
6 Preheat grill. Sprinkle cassoulet with breadcrumbs; place under grill until breadcrumbs are browned lightly.
7 Meanwhile, make spring onion couscous. Serve cassoulet with couscous.

spring onion couscous Place stock in medium saucepan; bring to the boil. Remove from heat, stir in couscous and butter, cover; stand about 5 minutes or until stock is absorbed, fluffing with fork occasionally. Add onion; toss gently to combine.

nutritional count per serving 66.8g total fat (23.5g saturated fat); 5267kJ (1260 cal); 65.6g carbohydrate; 90.7g protein; 19.3g fibre

slow cooker: suitable to the end of step 5
suitable to freeze at the end of step 4

SLOW-COOKED DUCK
WITH CABBAGE AND FENNEL

prep + cook time 2¾ hours **serves** 4

½ small red cabbage (600g),
cut into four wedges
1 large leek (500g),
chopped coarsely
4 baby fennel bulbs (520g),
trimmed, halved lengthways
1 tablespoon fresh rosemary leaves
2 cloves garlic, sliced thinly
1 cup (250ml) chicken stock
⅓ cup (80ml) cider vinegar
2 tablespoons redcurrant jelly
4 duck leg portions (1.2kg),
trimmed
1 tablespoon salt

balsamic-roasted potatoes
10 small potatoes (1kg), halved
30g butter, melted
2 tablespoons balsamic vinegar

1 Preheat oven to 160°C/140°C fan-assisted.
2 Combine cabbage, leek, fennel, rosemary, garlic, stock, vinegar and jelly in medium deep baking dish. Rub duck skin with salt; place duck, skin-side up, on cabbage mixture. Cook, uncovered, in oven, about 2¼ hours or until duck meat is tender and skin crisp.
3 Meanwhile, make balsamic-roasted potatoes.
4 Strain pan juices through muslin-lined sieve into medium saucepan; cover duck and cabbage mixture to keep warm. Skim fat from surface of pan juices; bring to the boil. Boil, uncovered, about 5 minutes or until sauce thickens slightly.
5 Serve duck with cabbage mixture and balsamic-roasted potatoes; drizzle with sauce.

balsamic-roasted potatoes Combine potatoes, butter and vinegar in medium baking dish. Roast, uncovered, alongside duck, about 1¼ hours or until potatoes are tender and browned lightly, brushing potatoes occasionally with vinegar mixture in dish.

nutritional count per serving 61.7g total fat (20.5g saturated fat); 3783kJ (905 cal); 50.3g carbohydrate; 31.5g protein; 14.5g fibre

slow cooker: suitable to the end of step 2
not suitable to freeze

BRAISED SWEET GINGER DUCK

prep + cook time 2 hours **serves** 4

1.8kg whole duck
3 cups (750ml) water
½ cup (125ml) chinese cooking wine
⅓ cup (80ml) japanese soy sauce
¼ cup (55g) firmly packed light brown sugar
1 whole star anise
3 spring onions, halved
3 cloves garlic, quartered
10cm piece fresh ginger (50g), unpeeled, chopped coarsely
2 teaspoons sea salt
1 teaspoon five-spice powder
750g baby bok choy, halved

1 Preheat oven to 180°C/160°C fan-assisted.
2 Discard neck from duck, wash duck; pat dry, inside and out, with absorbent paper. Score duck in thickest parts of skin; cut duck in half through breastbone and along both sides of backbone, discard backbone. Tuck wings under duck.
3 Place duck, skin-side down, in medium shallow baking dish; add the combined water, cooking wine, sauce, sugar, star anise, onion, garlic and ginger. Cover; cook, in oven, about 1 hour or until duck is cooked through.
4 Increase oven temperature to 220°C/200°C fan-assisted. Remove duck from braising liquid in pan; strain liquid through muslin-lined sieve into large saucepan. Place duck, skin-side up, on wire rack in same baking dish. Rub combined salt and five-spice all over duck; roast duck, uncovered, in oven about 30 minutes or until skin is crisp.
5 Discard fat from surface of braising liquid; bring to the boil. Reduce heat; simmer, uncovered, 10 minutes. Add bok choy; simmer, covered, 5 minutes or until bok choy is just tender.
6 Cut duck halves into two pieces; divide bok choy, braising liquid and duck among serving plates.

nutritional count per serving 105.7g total fat (31.7g saturated fat); 4974kJ (1190 cal); 17.9g carbohydrate; 40.8g protein; 3.5g fibre

slow cooker: not suitable
not suitable to freeze

glossary

bok choy also known as chinese white cabbage; has a fresh, mild mustard taste. Use both stems and leaves, stir-fried or braised. Baby bok choy is much smaller and more tender than bok choy.

butternut squash sometimes used interchangeably with the word pumpkin, butternut squash is a member of the gourd family. Various types can be substituted for one another.

cardamom can be bought in pod, seed or ground form. Has a distinctive, aromatic, sweetly rich flavour.

char siu sauce a Chinese barbecue sauce made from sugar, water, salt, fermented soya bean paste, honey, soy sauce, malt syrup and spices. Available from Chinese supermarkets and online.

cheese

parmesan a sharp-tasting, dry, hard cheese, made from skimmed or semi-skimmed milk and aged for at least a year.

pecorino a hard, sheep's- or cow's-milk cheese. Straw-coloured and grainy in texture, it's mainly used for grating. Parmesan can be substituted.

ricotta a soft, sweet, moist, white, cow-milk cheese with a low fat content (about 8.5 per cent) and a slightly grainy texture. The name roughly translates as 'cooked again' and refers to ricotta's manufacture from a whey that is itself a by-product of other cheese making.

chickpeas also called garbanzos, hummus or channa; an irregularly round, sandy-coloured legume.

cinnamon dried inner bark of the shoots of the cinnamon tree. Available as a stick or ground.

coconut

cream available in tins and cartons; as a rule, the proportions are two parts coconut to one part water.

milk unsweetened coconut milk available in cans. A light version is also available.

coriander

dried a fragrant herb; coriander seeds and ground coriander must never be used to replace fresh coriander or vice versa. The tastes are completely different.

fresh bright-green-leafed herb with a pungent flavour.

cornflour also known as cornstarch; used as a thickening agent in cooking.

couscous a fine, grain-like cereal product, made from semolina.

cream we used fresh cream in this book, unless otherwise stated. Also known as pure cream and pouring cream; has no additives unlike commercially thickened cream. Minimum fat content 35%.

soured a thick commercially-cultured soured cream. Minimum fat content 35%.

bok choy

shitake mushroom

cumin available both ground and as whole seeds; cumin has a warm, earthy, rather strong flavour.

fennel bulb vegetable, also known as finocchio or anise. Also the name given to dried seeds having a liquorice flavour.

fenugreek a member of the pea family, the seeds have a bitter taste; the ground seeds are a traditional ingredient in Indian curries, powders and pastes.

fish sauce also called nam pla or nuoc nam; made from pulverised salted fermented fish, mostly anchovies. Has a pungent smell and strong taste; use sparingly.

five-spice powder a fragrant mixture of ground cinnamon, cloves, star anise, sichuan pepper and fennel seeds.

garam masala a blend of spices based on varying proportions of cardamom, cinnamon, cloves, coriander, fennel and cumin, roasted and ground together.

Black pepper and chilli can be added for a hotter version.

ginger

fresh also called green or root ginger; the thick gnarled root of a tropical plant. Can be kept, peeled, covered with dry sherry in a jar and refrigerated, or frozen in an airtight container.

ground also known as powdered ginger; used as a flavouring in cakes and pies but cannot be substituted for fresh ginger.

harissa a North African paste made from dried red chillies, garlic, olive oil and caraway seeds; can be used as a rub for meat, an ingredient in sauces and dressings, or eaten on its own as a condiment. It is available, ready-made, from Middle-Eastern food shops and some supermarkets.

kaffir lime leaves aromatic leaves used fresh or dried in Asian dishes.

moroccan seasoning available from most Middle-Eastern food stores, spice shops and major supermarkets. Turmeric, cinnamon and cumin add authentic Moroccan flavouring to dishes.

mushrooms

button small, cultivated white mushrooms having a delicate, subtle flavour.

chestnut light to dark brown mushrooms with mild, earthy flavour.

oyster also known as abalone; grey-white mushrooms shaped like a fan. Prized for their smooth texture and subtle, oyster-like flavour.

portobello mature chestnut mushrooms. Large, dark brown mushrooms with full-bodied flavour; ideal for filling or barbecuing.

shiitake cultivated fresh mushroom; has a rich, meaty flavour.

mustard, dijon a pale brown, distinctively flavoured fairly mild French mustard.

orzo small, rice-shaped pasta used in soups and salads.

palm sugar also called nam tan pip, jaggery, jawa or gula melaka; made from the sap of the sugar palm tree. Light brown to black in colour; usually sold in rock-hard cakes. If unavailable, use brown sugar. Available from some supermarkets and Asian food stores.

palm sugar

star anise

pancetta an Italian salt-cured pork roll, usually cut from the belly; used, chopped, in cooked dishes to add flavour. Bacon can be substituted.

paprika ground dried red pepper; available sweet, smoked or hot. Sweet paprika is available at delis, speciality food stores and online.

passata thick sauce made from puréed tomatoes.

pearl barley the husk is removed, then hulled and polished so that the 'pearl' of the original grain remains, much the same as white rice.

polenta a flour-like cereal made of ground corn; similar to cornmeal but finer and lighter in colour; also the name of the dish made from it.

preserved lemon a North African specialty, the citrus is preserved, usually whole, in a mixture of salt and lemon juice or oil. To use, remove and discard pulp, squeeze juice from rind, then rinse rind well before slicing thinly. Available from specialty food shops and delicatessens.

ras el hanout is a classic spice blend used in Moroccan cooking. The name means 'top of the shop' and is the very best spice blend that a spice merchant has to offer. The blends may often contain more than 20 different spices.

redcurrant jelly sweet condiment made from redcurrants; commonly served with lamb or venison.

sesame oil made from roasted, crushed, white sesame seeds; a flavouring rather than a cooking medium.

soy sauce also known as sieu, is made from fermented soya beans. Several variations are available in most supermarkets and Asian food stores. We use a mild Japanese variety in our recipes; possibly the best table soy and the one to choose if you only want one variety.

light soy a fairly thin, pale but salty tasting sauce; used in dishes in which the natural colour of the ingredients is to be maintained. Not to be confused with salt-reduced or low-sodium soy sauces.

star anise the dried, star-shaped seed pod can be used whole as a flavouring and the seeds used alone as a spice; both can be used ground. While it does have a slight liquorice-like taste, it should not be compared to or confused with anise, being far more spicily pungent, with overtones of clove and cinnamon. Available from most supermarkets.

vanilla

extract obtained from vanilla beans infused in water; a non-alcoholic version of essence.

pod dried long, thin pod from a tropical golden orchid grown in central and South America and Tahiti; the minuscule black seeds inside the bean are used to impart a distinctively sweet vanilla flavour.

vinegar

balsamic authentic only from the province of Modena, Italy; made from a regional wine of white trebbiano grapes specially processed then aged in antique wooden casks to give the exquisite pungent flavour.

cider made from fermented apples.

malt made from fermented malt and beech shavings.

white wine based on fermented white wine.

vanilla pod

index

[index]
127

conversion charts

measures

One metric tablespoon holds 20ml; one metric teaspoon holds 5ml.

All cup and spoon measurements are level. The most accurate way of measuring dry ingredients is to weigh them. When measuring liquids, use a clear glass or plastic jug with metric markings.

We use large eggs with an average weight of 60g.

dry measures

METRIC	IMPERIAL
15g	½oz
30g	1oz
60g	2oz
90g	3oz
125g	4oz (¼lb)
155g	5oz
185g	6oz
220g	7oz
250g	8oz (½lb)
280g	9oz
315g	10oz
345g	11oz
375g	12oz (¾lb)
410g	13oz
440g	14oz
470g	15oz
500g	16oz (1lb)
750g	24oz (1½lb)
1kg	32oz (2lb)

liquid measures

METRIC	IMPERIAL
30ml	1 fluid oz
60ml	2 fluid oz
100ml	3 fluid oz
125ml	4 fluid oz
150ml	5 fluid oz
190ml	6 fluid oz
250ml	8 fluid oz
300ml	10 fluid oz
500ml	16 fluid oz
600ml	20 fluid oz
1000ml (1 litre)	32 fluid oz

length measures

METRIC	IMPERIAL
3mm	⅛in
6mm	¼in
1cm	½in
2cm	¾in
2.5cm	1in
5cm	2in
6cm	2½in
8cm	3in
10cm	4in
13cm	5in
15cm	6in
18cm	7in
20cm	8in
23cm	9in
25cm	10in
28cm	11in
30cm	12in (1ft)

oven temperatures

These are fan-assisted temperatures. If you have a conventional oven (ie. not fan-assisted), increase temperatures by 10–20°.

	°C (CELSIUS)	°F (FAHRENHEIT)	GAS MARK
Very low	100	210	½
Low	130	260	1–2
Moderately low	140	280	3
Moderate	160	325	4–5
Moderately hot	180	350	6
Hot	200	400	7–8
Very hot	220	425	9